Alice's Diary

LIVING WITH DIABETES

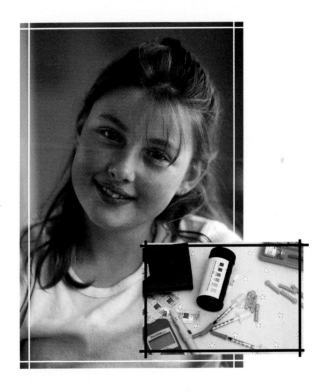

MARIE GIBSON
PHOTOGRAPHS BY LLOYD PARK

Learning Media

Contents

Tuesday, April 6

I think there's something wrong with me. I'm so thirsty all the time, and I keep needing to go to the bathroom. Last night, I had to get up five times.

Mom's getting mad with me because I don't want to eat. I just want more and more to drink. She says I'm not leaving

enough room for good food. She even put the milk away at breakfast so I wouldn't have any more, but as soon as she left the room, I helped myself. I felt kind of guilty, but I couldn't help it. I felt like I'd been running in the sun!

Wednesday, April 7

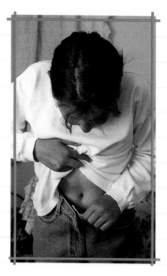

Today's been unbelievable. It all started with my old jeans — I put them on this morning, and instead of being too tight, like they used to be, there was enough room for both hands inside my belt.

Mom said that that proved I wasn't eating enough and she was going to take me to the doctor. Then I threw up! She made an appointment right away.

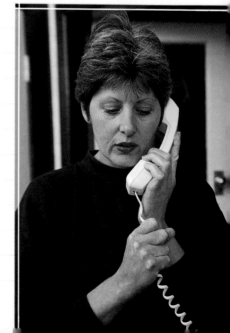

At the doctor's, Mom told him all about me drinking a lot and going to the bathroom all the time. He asked me to go right then — in a jar! Then he dipped a strip of paper in it, and the paper went brown. He said that meant there was sugar in my urine. The nurse pricked my finger with a little gadget that tested my blood. The screen said HI.

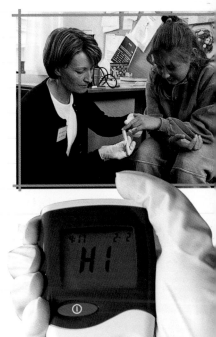

That's when the doctor told me I had **diabetes.** He said the tests showed I had way too much sugar in my blood, which meant my pancreas – whatever that is – wasn't working properly to make something called insulin.

What Is Diabetes?

Having diabetes means there is too much glucose (a kind of sugar) in your blood.

If your blood glucose is too high, you:
- feel tired and thirsty
- need to go to the bathroom often
- lose weight.

If your blood glucose gets very high, you feel sick and cross and may throw up.

In the United States, the United Kingdom, Australia, and New Zealand, about 15 out of every 100,000 children get diabetes every year.

Insulin

The pancreas is a gland behind your stomach that makes insulin. Insulin controls the level of glucose in your blood.

It does this by making sure that the glucose from the food you eat goes into your muscles and all the other parts of your body that need it. If your pancreas stops making insulin, glucose can't get out of your bloodstream to do its work. So it builds up there until you become sick.

I felt awful. There really WAS something wrong with me! I thought the doctor would give me some pills or something to make it better, but he told Mom she'd have to take me to the local hospital.

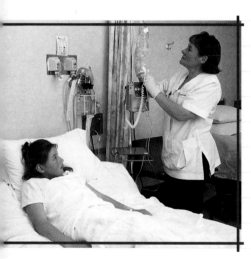

At the hospital, they put a tube into a vein in the back of my hand and connected it to a plastic bag full of stuff called **saline.** Then they took another blood test. This time, the meter read 420 instead of HI. I thought that must be good news – till the nurse told me it should be about 150.

WHAT DO THE TEST RESULTS MEAN?

Test Meter Reading	What It Means
35	Your blood glucose is extremely low. You could become unconscious. You need urgent medical attention.
55 to 65	Your blood glucose is low. You may have a headache and need encouragement to eat or drink. You should take fast-acting glucose.
75	Your blood glucose is slightly low. You need food.
100 to 150	Normal level
180	Maximum normal level
360	Your blood glucose is getting very high.
540	This is as high as some meters will measure. If your blood glucose gets this high, you need medical help.

They said I had to go in an ambulance to the City Hospital, where there's a special **diabetes clinic**. I was really upset when I heard that. Mom was worried, too. But then the **diabetes educator**, Lyn, came and talked to us. She helped me to understand what diabetes is. She said I'd be fine once they got it under control.

So now I'm here, in the City Hospital. Mom's here with me. I don't feel as bad now as I did when I first got the news. But I'm

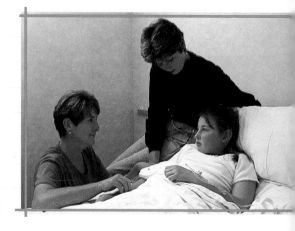

still not crazy about having diabetes. I hope we get it under control SOON.

Thursday, April 8

This sure is a big hospital! There are miles of corridors, and elevators everywhere.

I wasn't allowed anything to eat last night. The nurses explained that some foods – called carbohydrates – turn to sugar when they're digested, and I already had too much sugar in my blood.

CARBOHYDRATES

Bread, cereal, cookies, rice, pasta, fruit, candy, starchy vegetables like potatoes and corn, and dairy products such as milk, ice cream, and yogurt are all carbohydrates. They are the energy foods, which are converted to glucose when they are digested. The glucose is fed into our blood, which carries it to every part of the body. Glucose is the "fuel" that keeps our bodies working. Just being alive uses up this fuel, but exercise – like walking, running, and swimming – uses it up more quickly.

Then, I hardly got any sleep because nurses came every hour to test my blood sugar level.

Early this morning, a doctor came and told me I could have breakfast right after I'd had some insulin. I was getting kind of hungry by then, so that sounded like a good idea – until the nurse came in with a needle! I guess I made a fuss, but the nurse was nice. She sat on the bed and told me what insulin was and why I had to have it. So I let her give me the shot. It wasn't so bad.

I had another one before supper this evening. I guess it's just sinking in that I've got diabetes for keeps. I'm going to have to have at least two shots every day for THE REST OF MY LIFE.

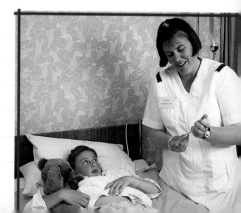

Monday, April 12

It's OK in the hospital, except for the shots. I've gotten heaps of gifts. Dad brought me a radio and some blue pajamas with moons and stars on them. The nurses gave me a bear. Every day I go to the schoolroom with the other kids, but we don't have to do much schoolwork. Today, I did paintings and made a model.

This morning, Mom learned how to give me my shots, and I did my own blood sugar test.

This afternoon, the **dietitian** came to talk to me. She said that I have to try to eat the same amounts of food at the same times each day so that my

blood sugar balances the insulin from my shots. I can't just eat whatever I want whenever I feel like it anymore. The dietitian said that sweet things like chocolate and soda are only for SPECIAL TREATS. Mostly, I should eat things from the Healthy Food Pyramid — but the same goes for everyone, she said, not just people with diabetes.

It's all kind of a drag. But at least I'm feeling better now — more like myself again.

BALANCING THE SEESAW

Keeping diabetes under control is all about balancing food and exercise with insulin.

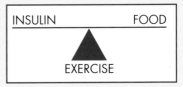

If all three are at a normal level, you are "balanced." A change in any one of the three will upset the balance. For example, if you have more exercise than usual, you will need either more food or less insulin to keep the balance.

THE HEALTHY FOOD PYRAMID

Soda, candy, fried food, ice cream
– occasional treats only

Meat, chicken, fish, beans, nuts, eggs
– 1 serving a day

Milk, cheese, yogurt
– 2 servings a day

Fruit and vegetables
– 5 servings a day

Bread and cereals
– 6 servings a day

Thursday, April 15

Back home at last! I had lots of stuff to bring with me – **syringes** and needles, a blood glucose test kit, a **logbook** to record my test results, and all my presents. I've got a Medic Alert bracelet too so that if I ever have an accident and can't talk, the ambulance people will know I have diabetes.

I didn't go to school today. I had to try out the daily timetable they gave me in the hospital. I have to have my shots at the same time every morning and evening and do a test before each meal.

DAILY TIMETABLE

7:55 A.M.	Test and shot
8:00 A.M.	Breakfast
10:40 A.M.	Snack
12:30 P.M.	Test and lunch
3:00 P.M.	Snack
5:50 P.M.	Test and shot
6:00 P.M.	Supper
8:45 P.M.	Test and snack
9:00 P.M.	Bed

Lyn, the diabetes educator, came to see me this afternoon. She talked about hypoglycemia and hyperglycemia. It's all kind of confusing.

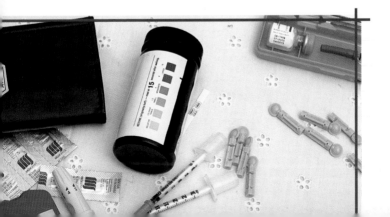

HYPERGLYCEMIA

Hyperglycemia is when blood glucose is too high. You are always thirsty, go to the bathroom often, feel sleepy, and lose weight. You need to see a **health professional**.

CAUSES OF HYPERGLYCEMIA

- Not enough insulin
- Too much food
- Less exercise than usual

HYPOGLYCEMIA

Hypoglycemia happens when blood sugar gets low – below 75 on the test meter. You might feel dizzy and sweaty. Without food, your blood glucose will get lower still, and your brain will not get enough glucose. You won't be able to think properly, and you may not be able to walk straight.

If your blood glucose gets very low, you may black out. You will need an **injection** of **glucagon**, which will raise the blood glucose fast so that you can then have something to eat.

CAUSES OF HYPOGLYCEMIA

- Too much insulin
- Not enough food – maybe missing a meal
- More exercise than usual

HYPERGLYCEMIA

HYPERGLYCEMIA
Very high blood glucose

HIGH

HIGH blood glucose

More food than usual	Not enough insulin	Less exercise than usual

NORMAL BLOOD GLUCOSE LEVEL

NORMAL

FOOD | **INSULIN** | **EXERCISE**

Less food than usual	Too much insulin	More exercise than usual

LOW

LOW blood glucose

HYPOGLYCEMIA

Very low blood glucose
HYPOGLYCEMIA

Monday, April 19

It was my first day back at school on Friday. It was cool to see everyone, but ... it turns out there was a bug going around, and wouldn't you know it, I picked it up. My first test this morning was too high even though I hadn't eaten much. Mom called Lyn. She brought some fast-acting insulin. She told us to test every two hours, drink lots, and ring her so she could check how things were going. The tests came down bit by bit.

Thursday, April 22

I did my own shot tonight! I had to go to the diabetes clinic in the city this morning, and the doctor there gave me a special injection pen. It's easier to use than a syringe, so Mom doesn't have to do my shots anymore.

Friday, April 23

We had PE at school today. I was in the cross-country. I remembered to have a snack before we started, like Lyn told me. But when we got back, I flopped down on the grass, and my friend Angela said I looked a bit pale.

I said I felt all right, but she made me do a test anyway. My hands shook a bit as I got the kit out.

Sure enough, my blood sugar was down to 70. I ate some of my emergency candy. Angela was really good. She made me sit down and eat the last sandwich from my lunchbox, and then she went for the teacher. He wanted to send me home, but I felt OK after a few minutes. I did another test, and it was back up to 100. It's good to have a friend like Angela.

Monday, April 26

A weird thing happened today – another girl in my class, Tracy, has just found out

she has diabetes too. She's in the hospital, probably feeling scared like I was. Maybe I'll be able to help her when she gets back.

Wednesday, May 5

Tracy came home from the hospital today. Mom invited her and her mom around for coffee. Our mothers talked and talked about food and tests and stuff like that. Tracy and I talked about having shots and looked at each other's logbooks.

I asked Tracy to come to the school dance on Saturday with me and Angela. Tracy's mom phoned Lyn to ask her what we should do about food. Lyn said to keep away from the sweet things and have sandwiches or stuff like that instead. We're going to take some diet soda.

Saturday, May 8

The dance last night was great! Everyone danced and sang like crazy. The gym got really hot – so did we. The only problem was, the supper was late. I was feeling a bit shaky by the time it arrived, and even after I'd had a sandwich, I didn't feel much better. I started sweating and trembling. Tracy came out to the kitchen

with me, and we both did a test. Tracy's was all right, but mine was way down to 55, so I ate my glucose candy. I felt a bit better after that.

Mom made me do another test when I got home. It was better (90) but still too low, so I had a big snack. At last the test was normal, and I went to bed.

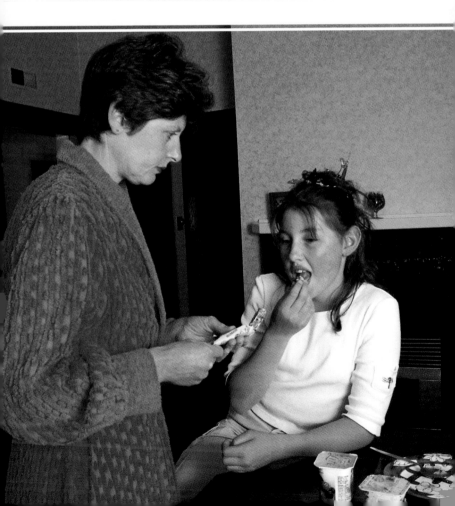

The next thing
I knew, Mom was
waking me up. It was
3:30 A.M. She was
worried and wanted
me to do another test
because my blood
sugar goes down
during the night when
I'm not eating. Sure
enough, it was back
down to 55. I had to
have some candy – in
the middle of the
night! At breakfast,

my test was back up to normal.

When we told Lyn what had happened,
she said that I'd had a "delayed hypo"
because I'd had much more exercise than
usual. She said that the next time I went
to a dance, I should have less insulin to
balance the exercise.

Wednesday, May 26

Lyn's organizing a camp for kids with diabetes later in the year – cool! Tracy and I are both planning to go. Lyn says it'll be just like other camps except there'll be people who know all about diabetes there to help us if we need it.

It's been more than two weeks since the dance, and I haven't gotten out of balance again. If I remember to have an extra snack before PE, to counter the exercise, I'm fine.

I remember when I first found out that I had diabetes I felt like some kind of freak. But it doesn't really bother me now that I've gotten used to it. I'm still just a regular kid after all!

Glossary

(These words are printed in bold type
the first time they appear in the book.)

diabetes: a condition where the pancreas stops
making insulin

diabetes clinic: a place in the hospital where
patients with diabetes are treated

diabetes educator: a health professional who
helps patients with their diabetes

dietitian: a health professional who helps people
with their diet

glucagon: a substance made in the pancreas that
has the opposite effect to insulin – it puts
more glucose into the blood

health professional: a doctor, nurse, or someone
with similar training

injection: a shot or a jab from a syringe

logbook: a book for keeping a record of blood
test results

saline: salt and water

syringe: a medical instrument for injecting fluids
into the body

Index